D0811044

# Purple Ronnie's
## Little Guide to your
# New Baby

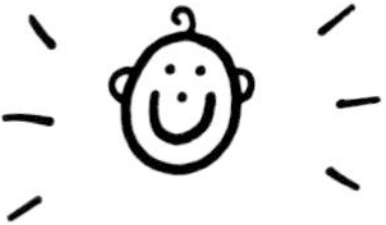

by Purple Ronnie

First published 2004 by Boxtree
an imprint of Pan Macmillan Ltd
Pan Macmillan, 20 New Wharf Road, London N1 9RR
Basingstoke and Oxford
Associated companies throughout the World
www.panmacmillan.com

ISBN 0 7522 7272 1

9 8 7 6 5 4 3 2

A CIP catalogue record for this book is available from
the British Library.

Text by Giles Andreae
Illustrations by Janet Cronin
Printed and bound in Hong Kong

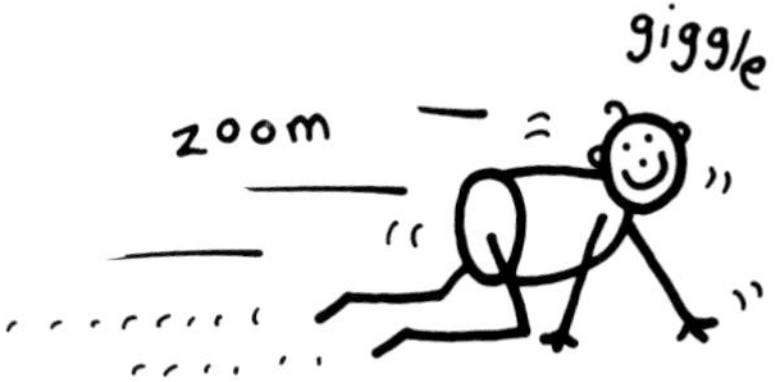
giggle
zoom

# Being Pregnant

The best thing about being pregnant is that you can spend 9 months being bonkers and your partner is meant to be nice to you the whole time

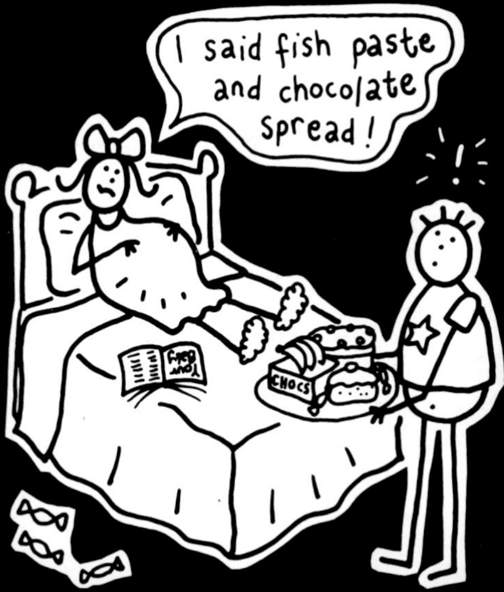
I said fish paste and chocolate spread!
Your diary
CHOCS

# Shopping

Babies' clothes make girls go so gooey that it is hard not to end up with loads more than you need

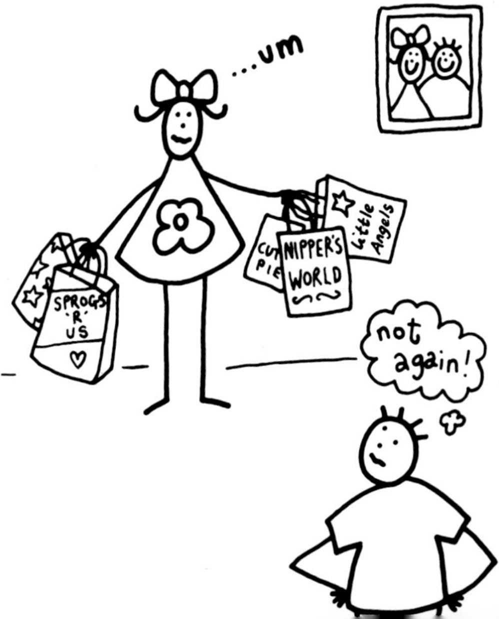
...um
SPROGS 'R' US
NIPPER'S WORLD
Little Angels
not again!

# Your Car

It is now time to buy the kind of car that all your friends will tease you about

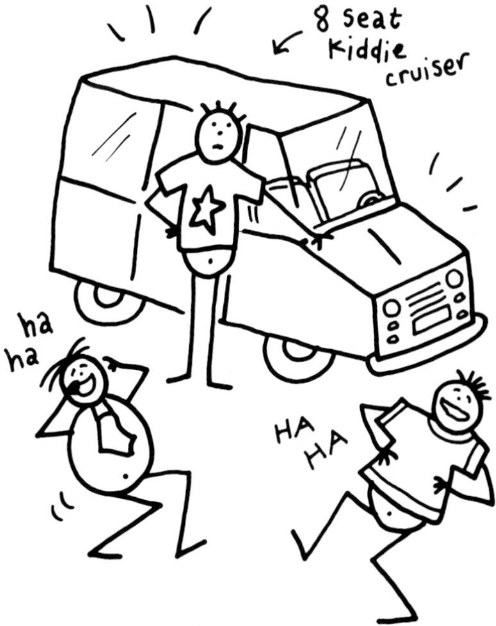
8 seat
kiddie
cruiser
ha
ha
HA
HA

# Having Your Baby

Everyone knows that having a baby is the most painful thing in the universe

☆ There are some quite good ways of dealing with this

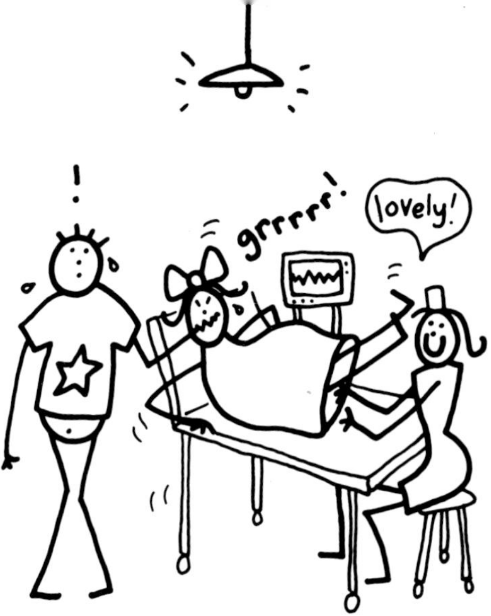
grrrrr!
lovely!

# Your New Baby

Even though your new baby will look like a shrivelled-up prune, you will think it is the most beautiful thing in the world

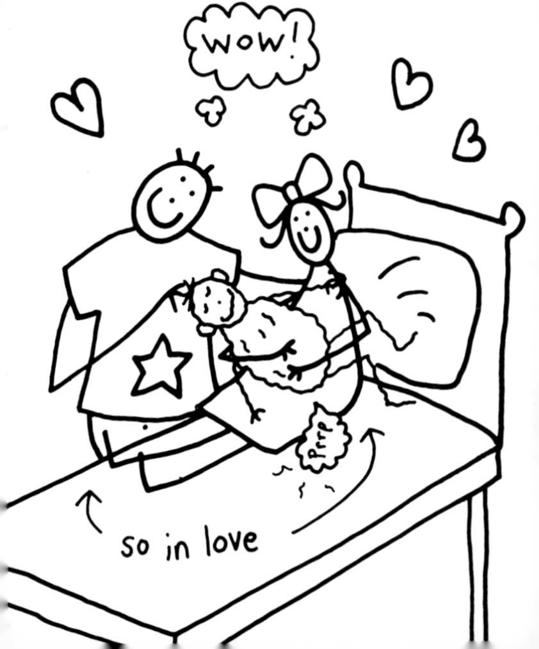
WOW!
Prrp
so in love

# Big Pants

You will now have to wear BIG PANTS for a while but you will be so blissed out that you won't mind at all

giggle

← huge
Mummy
Pants

# Baby Stuff

Even though new babies
are completely tiny,
the amount of stuff
they need is unbelievable

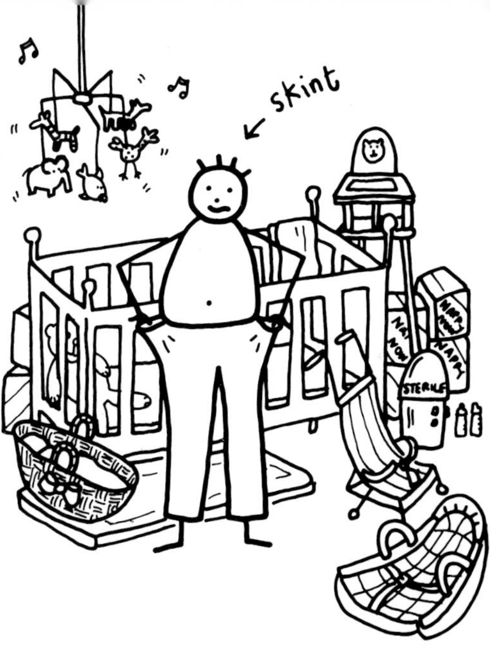
skint
NAPPY
STERILE

# Bosoms

After you have had your baby, your bosoms will suddenly get so enormous that you feel like they're going to explode

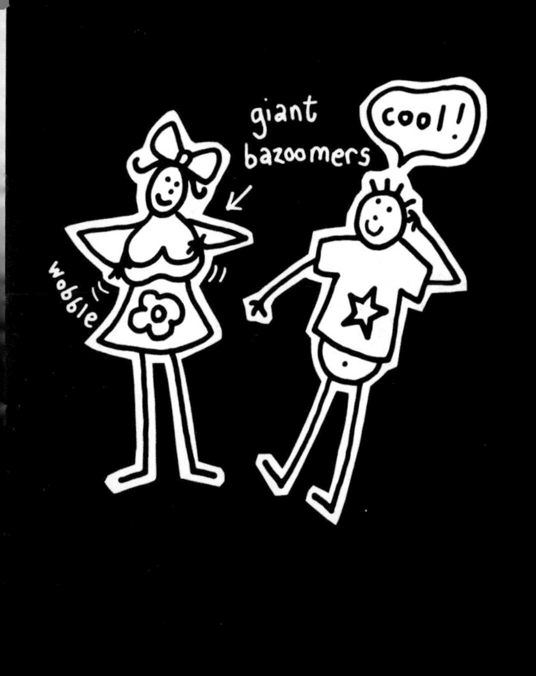
giant bazoomers
cool!
wobble

# The First Poo

It is almost impossible to imagine what comes out of your sweet little baby's bottom the first time it does a poo

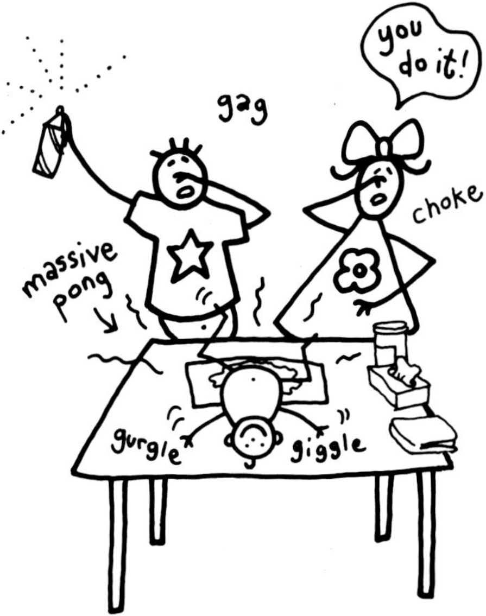
you do it!
gag
choke
massive pong
gurgle
giggle

# Crying

Babies have a special way of crying that feels like a hole is being drilled into your head

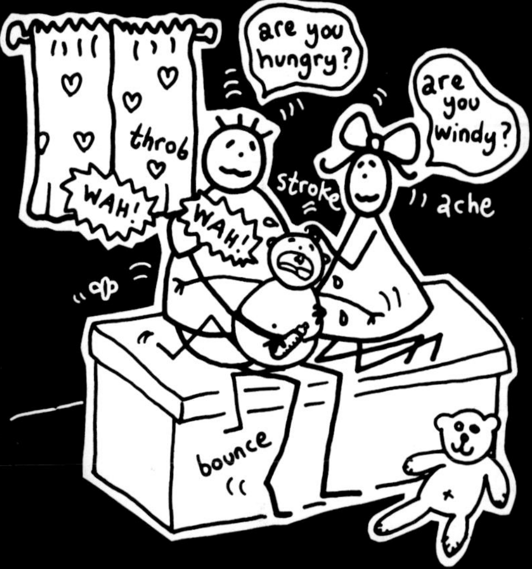
are you hungry?
are you windy?
throb
WAH!
WAH!
stroke
ache
bounce

# Car Seats

The first time you try to use a car seat you will go completely mad

<u>Warning</u>:- It never gets any easier

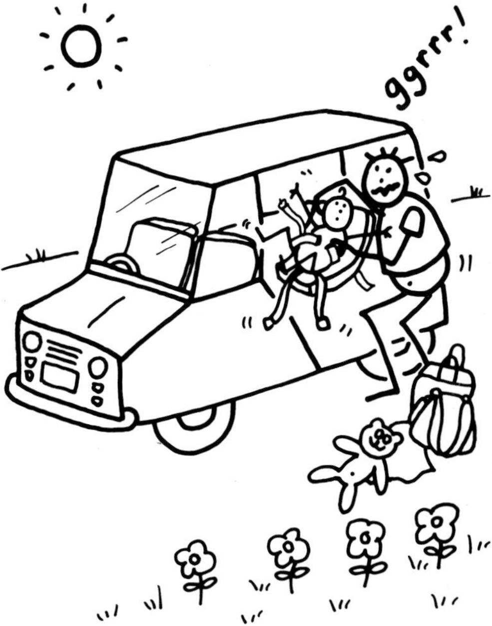
ggrrr!

# Baby Talk

Soon you will start talking in a way that no other person on earth could understand

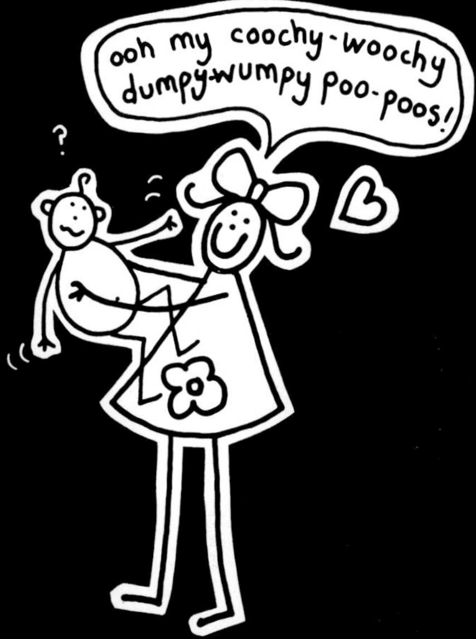
ooh my coochy-woochy dumpy-wumpy poo-poos!
?

# Smiling

It is hard to control your feelings the first time your baby smiles at you

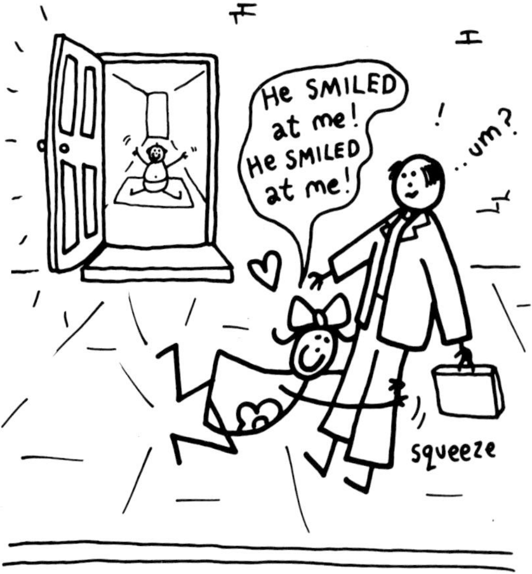
He SMILED at me! He SMILED at me!
! ...um?
squeeze

# Changing Nappies

Changing nappies is an art that men find hard to master

☆ Make sure they get loads of practice

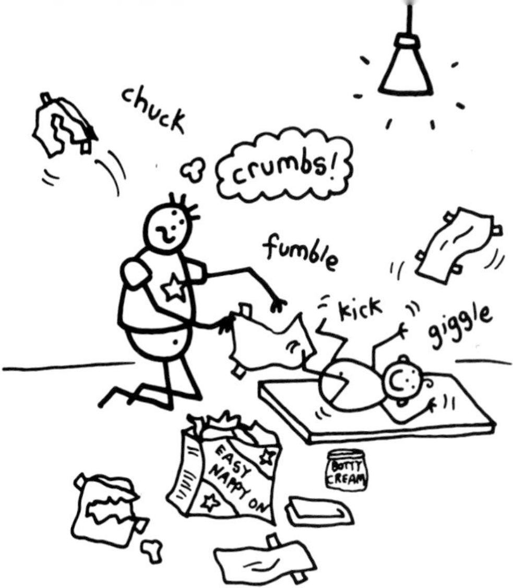

chuck
crumbs!
fumble
kick
giggle
EASY NAPPY ON
BOTTY CREAM

# Milk Brain

Sometimes after women have had a baby their brain goes a bit wobbly for a while

☆ Don't worry – this is perfectly normal

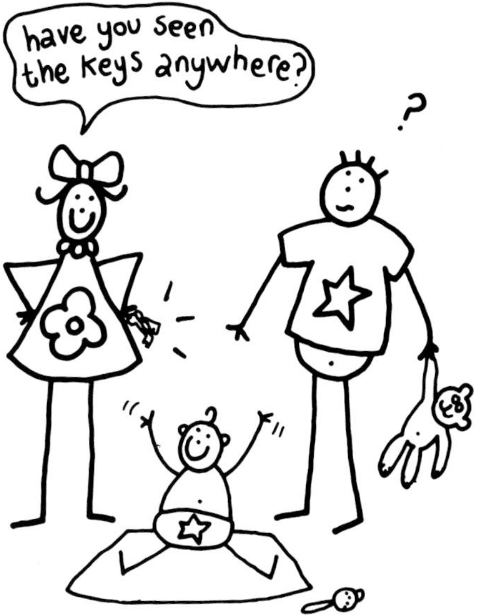
have you seen the keys anywhere?
?

# Other People

Beware- not everyone will think your new baby is as unbelievably interesting as you do

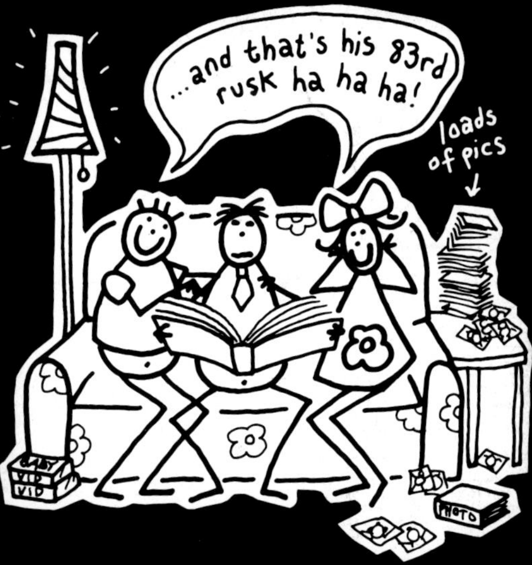
...and that's his 83rd rusk ha ha ha!
loads of pics
VID
VID
PHOTO

# Drinks

This will probably be the only time in your life when milk is even more important than booze

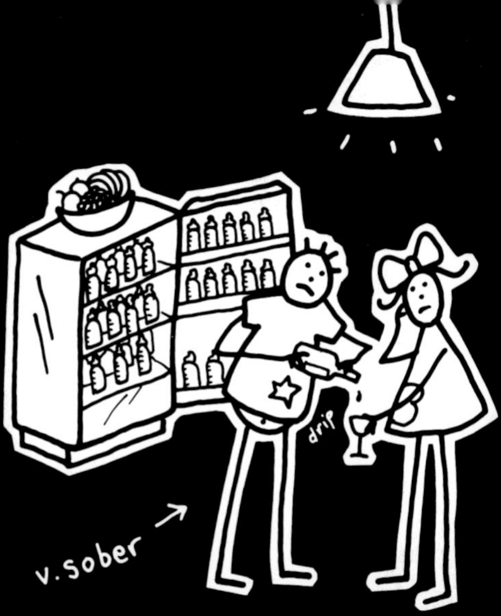
drip
v. sober

# Wee

## Warning:- the time babies like to wee the most is the minute you have taken their nappy off

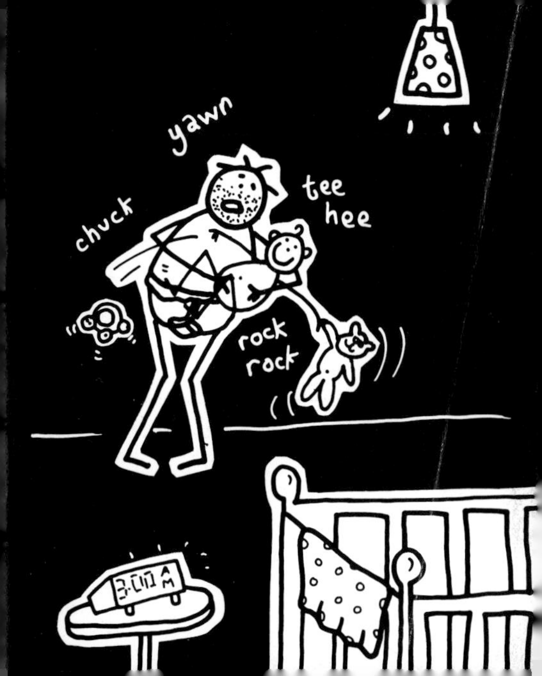
yawn
chuck
tee hee
rock rock
3:00 AM

# Tidiness

If you like things
to be tidy, it is best
to hide in the cupboard
for at least the
next 5 years

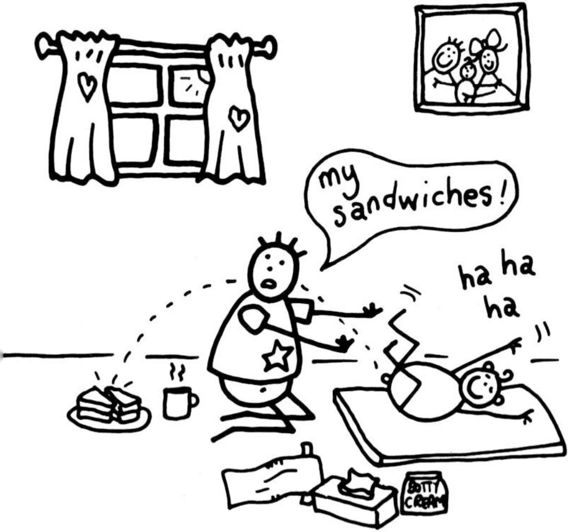
my sandwiches!
ha ha ha
BOTTY CREAM

# Sleeping

Babies are brilliant at picking the times when you are fast asleep to be most awake

# Sleeping

Babies are brilliant at picking the times when you are fast asleep to be most awake

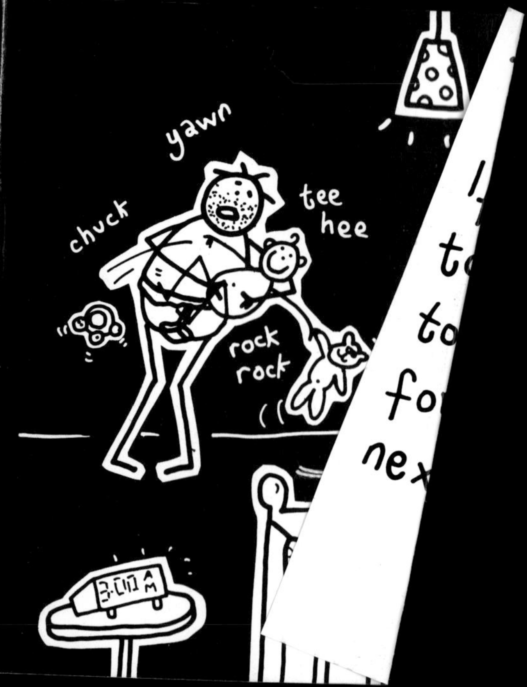

yawn
chuck
tee hee
rock rock

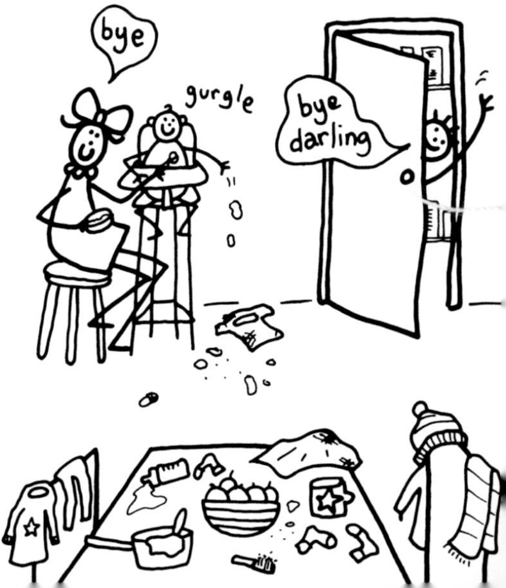
bye
gurgle
bye darling

# Sex

<u>Warning</u>:- You will both be too knackered to even think about Doing It for a long time

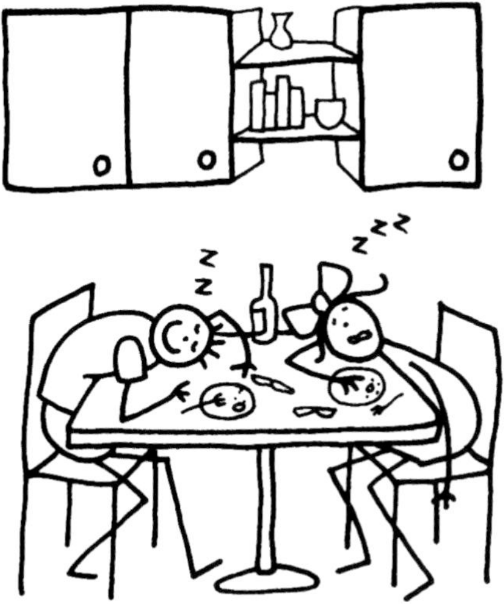

# More Babies

Even though babies are the hardest work in the world, some people just can't resist having more ...and more...and more!

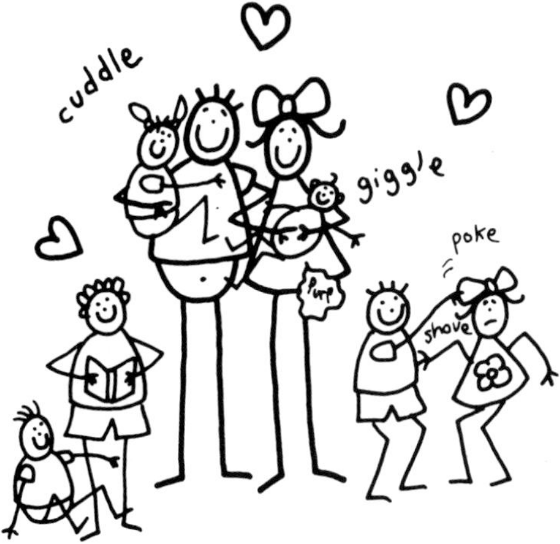
cuddle
giggle
Purp
poke
shove

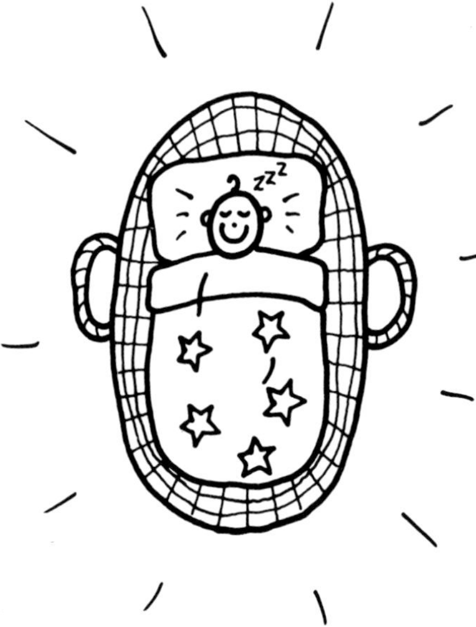